Knowing Enlightenment

Franklin Manickam

Franklyns Publications

Knowing Enlightenment

By

Franklin Manickam

Website: www.franklinmanickam.com
Email: info@franklinmanickam.com

Published & Printed by Franklyns Publications
202, John Rose CHS, Lady Fatima Road, Poisur, Kandivali west,
Mumbai 400067, India

ISBN: 978-93-5680-111-0

DEDICATION

I dedicate this book to my dear friends who are seeking enlightenment. Or even people who are not seeking it. My book aims to attract even people who are halfheartedly interested. I would like to thank existence for giving me a role of helping people achieve enlightenment.

I want to dedicate this book to those who have given hope, may my book give them hope.

To those who are sick. May they attain going beyond the sickness and towards the ultimate bliss.

I want to dedicate this book to you, the reader. May the lessons you discover on these pages leads you to enlightenment.

Finally, I want to dedicate to my father and mother Susai Manickam & Pushpam Manickam

Content

Part 1

Part 4

Introduction - How to read this book

'Knowing Enlightenment " is a guide to know yourself or to know the truth or become enlightened.

It is an effort to help someone who wants to be enlightened or to know the divine You must be reading this book to attain enlightenment or just checking for curiosity.

Whatever it may be existence has led you towards this reading and there would be a reason and it would be to make you move towards enlightenment.

While reading this book one needs to have an open view and not limit ourselves and to think openly without any crutches.

Before you read you need to have a clean slate or nothing in your mind open to new views. So that you can absorb what is new.

Things which will limit you will be your religious beliefs, your strong views from your past, your family upbringing and society upbringing.

You may also start questioning or comparing whether such views are there in your religious belief. You need to go beyond such thinking. Let yourself free and explore new views.

Without the old views dying you cannot know the new. And with the new you will progress and know the truth. With your old views you have not reached your destination. Now give an opportunity to the new

You have to attempt to take spiritual knowledge in a new way. With each generation there will always be some advancement in the thought process. Do take the jump into the new knowledge.

As you read this book, read it easily in a calm place. Maybe in a park or in your room alone without any disturbance.

When you read it again and again the same thing, the meaning will change every time you read it, because your mind is getting developed each time. After some time, there won't be any change in your thinking that is when you will know you have reached.

I have given concepts in a specific structure and going through each one in sequence will develop you overall.

\

"As you read this book, the first time you may understand something, when you re read it, you will understand something else, each time you read the meaning will change, it happens because you are growing. There will come a time when the meaning won't change any longer and then you have arrived"

- Franklin Manickam

Concept 1 - Who seeks enlightenment?

You must be having doubts about, out of the whole population who actually seeks enlightenment. What happens is that unless a person sees benefit in what he is doing, he may not seek a particular thing.

In this case of seeking enlightenment the person may have heard about it and may not know exactly what it is so who really seeks enlightenment. Generally, there are four types of people who actually seek enlightenment.

1. The first type of people are the seekers of knowledge.

They are these inquisitive people, who seek answers in everything they do in everyday life they might be doing various things and they question each and everything and unless they get a proper answer, may be in their work in everything, they do they question everything and a time comes when they seek god they want to know who is god. They want to know are the concepts related to God really true. Having all these questions in their mind they seek enlightenment, but it is not just the inquisitive people who seek enlightenment they are also very pious pure people who by their good deeds lead themselves to seek enlightenment so these are the first type of people the seeker of self-knowledge who seek enlightenment.

2. Now the second type of people are the ones who are very distressed.

The person may be distressed, maybe due to loss of someone in their family, maybe it is their mother, father, brother, wife, husband it could be anyone, or even maybe their lover. They must have been attached so much to that person and suddenly their loss has made them so depressed that they question the very existence of their life, such people seek answers to find peace because whatever they are doing to come out of that stress it's not helping. Now this is the moment where they have to seek answers. Unless they seek answers about the existence at this moment they will not be satisfied. To make themselves satisfied they will have to seek enlightenment.

Such people who also are quiet and pure by their good deeds lead to self-knowledge or enlightenment. Note there could be lots of people in distress, but unless they take a big step to know the truth it won't happen. A lot of people do lose their loved ones, but not all seek truth. You require some guidance at the right time and some karmas of their past which should help them.

3. **Now the third type of people who seek enlightenment are the seeker of wealth.**

Certain people who seek wealth have so much energy that they keep on making money, wealth or anything in abundance and they keep on winning in their life

These types of people at a certain point when they have enough, then they question whether earning wealth is satisfactory enough.

They may say "I have everything in abundance, but when I die it is of no use" they will question the very format of existence of birth and death. They would want to seek things which go beyond than what they have.

Some people also think of attaining immortality when such questions come, they seek knowledge of self or try to get enlightened, but again, there will be a lot of people who will be seeking but only those people who are unbiased and pure and by their good deed will try to attain it.

 And out of those people only some will actually succeed.

4. Now the fourth type of people, are the people who are a devotee of a particular god or deity or a religious person.

Who by their single-minded devotion are connected to the one deity they follow. And the connection becomes so deep they go so much inside their self that after a particular time they actually start knowing about enlightenment, but that happens after a long time but let me tell you this

These are the four types of people, but they are also pious and pure and have done a lot of good deed and existence help them towards enlightenment by their good deeds. Now the good deeds what they have done is not just about this life it could be about their past lives also.

Now what happens is that there are a lot of religions who don't believe in past life but the person's good deed of maybe 50, 60, 70 years of good deeds is just not enough there has to be a lot of things which has happened in the past and they have accumulated the good deeds and have reached to a particular stage whereby they seek enlightenment

So, these are the four types of people who seek enlightenment.

Concept 2 - People who don't seek enlightenment

I'll tell you about the people who don't seek enlightenment or the knowledge of self. These are the people who are ignorant whose focus is based on their ego or lust who take decisions by their ego and who don't take decisions by their pious neutral nature. They must be having different desires, maybe a desire of lust or of certain material things and maybe this person is more focused on their family. They'll be always focused on things which may not help them to get knowledge. Their focus is different and they will not seek enlightenment. But they will reach a stage after a lot of time where they will seek enlightenment existence for everybody keeps moving forward so maybe they may not seek now but they may seek later on. And it is not that if a person doesn't have their qualities to seek enlightenment they cannot. If they decide now, means right now, that they want to seek enlightenment, it will happen even if you don't have the quality to seek enlightenment. It will happen if you decide to seek making a desire decision to seek and making an effort towards it will get you closer to enlightenment and the existence will help you. Unless you decide to seek it will not never happen

Concept 3 - Soul & Transmigration of the soul.

Some look at the soul as a wonder without understanding anything. Some try to describe it but are unable. Some hear about it from people, but don't understand. Very few people of purity will actually understand. Just as we change clothes the individual soul takes repeated birth changing its body. Body changes but the soul or spirit or whatever name you give it remains as it, just as a watcher.

The soul watches its body changing from childhood to youth to old age to death.

Similarly, it also sees it acquiring another body after death.

All beings are unmanifest or invisible to our physical or body before and after death.

You may or not believe the transmigration theory or rebirth theory, but there are lot of facts which you can find out where there has been proof of re birth cases.

Also, there are various methods like hypnosis where you can go to your past life as well.

But you don't have to go through all the fact checking. Keep an open mind. Just remember this much, that the body is temporary and spirit doesn't change. As you further read the concepts it will become more and more clear.

Concept 4 - What is Soul or Spirit and body?

To know the soul or spirit one needs to go beyond the mind and body beyond the form which is a body and mind

The spirit or soul or God or the supreme spirit is formless which you cannot think about, which you cannot see, which you cannot hear which you cannot touch.

Generally, what happens is that people tend to believe in the soul or the spirit only when they talk about death. They have heard about it, they have heard about the soul that it is everlasting, but they don't really know about it.

People tend to believe in the soul only when there is a person who is dying or has died, they want to believe as a consolation that there is a soul and the person who has died still lives although the body has died

They want to believe that the soul of the person still lives. They want to believe that there is a next life, but they don't want to believe that there was a past life whereby the person has born in a particular family and has lived.

And has done good deeds or bad deeds and has died and they want to believe that there is a next life whereby they want to feel that even when they die, they will not actually die and their soul will keep living although many of the people and mostly all of them don't know what is the soul. To know the soul is very important, to know oneself to understand the spirit.

To know it, we simply have to divide ourselves into two parts. One part is which is a destructible part and the other part is which is the indestructible part of us. The destructible part is our body, mind and our senses, which when you're born keeps developing and then from a baby you become a youth, then you become an adult, and then you become old and the body dies. There is this indestructible part which we term it as a soul which sees all this happening.

The body grows and dies, but soul doesn't die. The body is born, but the soul is unborn the body ceases to exist, but the soul doesn't cease to exist, the body is not permanent but the soul is permanent and it cannot be destroyed.

Your body can be cut, but your soul cannot be cut.

Your body can be burned, but your soul cannot be burnt

Your body has form, but the soul doesn't have a form

Just as you change clothes, so does the soul changes different body after death based on the deeds which you have done.

Now there are different religions who believe in the next life and there are some religions who don't believe in the next life, but one needs to understand that unless the spirit takes a body after death how will it operate? How can be there be a personality of it?

All our desires and ambitions which our body and mind creates are not fulfilled and unless there is another body to fulfill it there seems to be something incomplete.

Another thing is that there are different people who are born in this world Some are born in rich family and some are born in a poor family. People born in a rich family, gets all the facilities and education to grow, whereas the person who was born in a poor family doesn't have all the facilities and their effort is always a struggle

It's easier for a person who is born in a family full of privileges and it's difficult for a person who is born in a family with less privileges.

It is important to understand the body, which will make you understand the soul which is diametrically opposite.

Concept 5 - How does nature choose different characteristic for different people?

So how does nature choose different characteristics for different people or privileges for different people. It is simply that if you have got different privileges in this life is simply because of the past deeds or the past deeds which are done in your previous life are yielding fruit in this life and that's the reason you got a family which helps you in your growth

There are other people who may be born in a poor family or in a family with less privileges whereby their life is a struggle so whatever deeds you're doing in this life; the fruits may yield in this life itself or it may yield in the next life.

If the deeds which you are doing are very sharp or intense, then it may yield fruit in this life itself otherwise it may get carried forward to the next life

Concept 6 - Knowing the soul or becoming enlightened is the same.

Knowing the soul or realizing the soul is the same as being enlightened.

To understand the soul, one needs to go from form to formless. The body has got form, but the spirit doesn't have form. God has no form, you cannot see it, you cannot taste it, you cannot touch it and you cannot think about it

To understand the soul or to realize the soul you need to actually experience it. And how do we experience the soul. To experience the soul. We need to go beyond our mind which is full of desires, anxieties ambitions and lust

Unless you go beyond these feelings, these desires you will not want to know about the soul and unless these desires are balanced and unless your mind is stable with balance, you will not be able to think about the soul or you won't be keen to know the soul.

A genuine inquiry is required, where you want to know the soul and want to go beyond the mind and the body and when you have that genuine inquiry you will find the soul. You need that hunger to know yourself or the soul and then you will know it. I telling you anything about the soul will not yield any result unless you try to find it

Because my hunger I can feel and I only can feed it, if you have hunger, you will only have to feed it. If you don't have the hunger, nothing can be done about it.

So, try to know the soul and make an effort and you will reach it. You need to go beyond the mind and to go beyond the mind is to be still and meditate to know your soul. It is a difficult process, but it is still not impossible because the soul is within you, you are the soul and if you go beyond your desires and ambitions and lust you will know it.

Concept 7 - Our Senses and Mind - How to master the Mind and the senses in your body

You have five bodily senses in your mind, which is why you seem to execute different things in your life.

1) Your sense of touch
2) Your sense of hearing
3) Your sense of sight
4) Your sense of taste and
5) Your sense of smell and on top of it you have your mind which controls all your senses

Knowing it very deeply will help you to know yourself. You must be having a craving for a certain kind of food, maybe it's chocolate, maybe it's different types of cuisine, but do you know the taste which comes in your tongue is directly connected to your brain or mind

Your mind is a storage of all your past experiences, you may have liked a certain kind of chocolate or a certain kind of food in your past and in your present or future, you may be craving for that particular thing and such senses are there in every human being.

Maybe they'd react in a different manner, but more or less it is the same reaction which you get so you may be thinking that I like a certain thing I like a particular food, but it is not that you like it. It is the senses and your mind which likes it you have a false impression that you like it but it is actually your senses and the mind that reacts in a certain manner

I can give you another example, maybe you are attracted to a particular person now in this case all your senses gets activated and your mind reacts in a certain manner and you say that "I like that person I am very much attracted to that person". It is nothing but your senses and mind which works in a particular manner in a programmed manner and you react in a certain way, so you need to understand that. You don't react but it is a combination of things which nature has created which creates a reaction.

All your five senses with your mind react in a certain manner and one needs to observe very minutely when your mind craves for a particular thing.

It generally happens that you are out of control of what you're going to do or you are automatically pulled towards a decision.

One needs to observe the mind very carefully at how it reacts and how it is programmed in a particular manner

One needs to see the mind or observe the mind very minutely or in a very detailed manner to understand how it functions

How there are preset things in your mind, which makes you react in a certain manner and unless you understand this and unless you see this you won't be able to master your mind

The senses and the mind are uncontrollable even for a very intelligent or a wise person unless you go beyond your mind your journey towards enlightenment will not happen.

Concept 8 - How do we master the mind?

For mastering the mind, the process is very simple, but yet very tough for some people. To master the mind, you don't need to control it, but you just need to observe the mind very carefully in a relaxed manner not stressing.

By observing how the mind reacts, how your senses reacts you will be able to master your mind. But observing needs to be done in a very detailed and relaxed manner. Because if you are not relaxed the mind is not relaxed, it's not possible without the mind in a neutral state.

You need to see how we are thinking what you are thinking, why you are thinking, how the senses are controlling you, how you react to a particular situation, why are you reacting in your subject in a certain manner.

Unless you see, unless you observe, very minutely you won't be able to master it and

I'm not saying that you need to control your mind or control your cravings

When you master your mind, you don't need to control anything all decisions taken when you master your mind will be proper and perfect.

 **Concept 9 - Can enlightenment be taught or told or can God be known.**

Enlightenment or knowing God or knowing the soul is the topmost principle or the first principle.

Enlightenment can only be experienced, and that experience cannot be told completely.

It is this reason when a mystic or a person who is enlightened when he speaks to people who are not enlightened, cannot really understand what they talk.

Because enlightenment is something to be experienced and does not have a form which could be explained.

It cannot be tasted.

It cannot be touched.

It cannot be smelled.

It cannot be seen.

It cannot be heard.

The human mind is a creation of the infinite energy and it is subpar to the infinite energy.

A subpar mind cannot experience the superior energy or God.

Only when the mind and its ego is destroyed.

Only then we can watch ourselves without prejudice and when we watch with no past or future thinking, only then we will come to the present and when we are totally in the present, we are close to enlightenment.

All the books or videos contain principles which are secondary, and not the primary thing for becoming enlightened.

These principles can lead you towards it, but unless you experience it yourself you will never know.

 ## Concept 10 - People avoid looking at nothingness inside

People are made up of their egos. Egos can be anything, any talent or anything they think they are good at. Maybe they are good at playing, maybe they are good looking, they may talk nicely, maybe they talk intelligently. These feelings make them fuller. But God or Godliness is at the exact opposite side. When you are empty, God appears or enlightenment happens.

People are afraid to become nothing. They want to keep changing to something. It could also be their religious rituals. All these things only make them full and there is no end to it.

The moment a person tries to look inside at his nothingness, he is fearful of losing his fullness or ego and the moment he hesitates, he loses the ones with the nothingness and enlightenment doesn't happen or God doesn't appear. The moment you disappear, God appears. And it is not that God comes, it is more that you come to know about it.

Concept 11 - In Joy or bliss, you disappear

With bliss, you tend to disappear, but will misery you are there thinking, your mind is active, working, trying to solve something. The moment the mind ceases to exist you tend to become afraid, that you may not exist, but when mind disappears a pure bliss appears which is Godliness.

At this very moment you can find bliss, but you won't do it because you have layers and layers of past which create obstacles.

Once you start being in the bliss you can do your day-to-day activities, but also be in bliss. You can watch what you are doing and when you are watching yourself whatever you do will be the right thing. Your inner bliss will also help you in your outward life. It will start reflecting.

Concept 12. The misguided have nothing but rituals

We can see people worshiping a particular deity, by doing some prayers and some steps of rituals. These are always for material benefits. The very idea that they are seeking material or health benefits does show their priority. Their priority is at the lower level of being materialistically satisfied. Only a person who is tired of the material things which keeps on getting changed. Seeks the thing that is Eternal, and no rituals can reach it. Only self-awareness, where the mind ceases to exist can they reach that stage

Concept 13. Modes of Nature

For our understanding we can divide the universe into two parts. 1.The eternal, unchanging and 2. Material nature which is changing and dynamic.

Material Nature has 3 modes.

1. The goodness mode

2. The passion mode

3. The ignorance mode.

In the goodness mode, a person is more compassionate and understanding to others.

In the passion mode you are more ambitious and self-achievement is your priority.

In the ignorance mode, a person is ignorant to what is right and keeps doing the wrong things which is harmful to self and society

Concept 14 - All works are works of Nature

Everything in this world has a certain momentum. Somehow nature pushes a certain person or a thing in its momentum. People do think they are doing things, but that's a very tiny effort they are doing. There is already a large force which pushes you to do things. Such momentum of material nature of how things are forced to happen, can be easily studied by the movement of planets and how during a certain phase or combination of planets things happen accordingly.

To find the combination of things which makes the thing happen is very difficult. But there is a logic of it.

At the most a person can control his actions which is again defined by the nature of the person which is predefined in a certain way. Watching all this happen a man who sees the nature as it is doesn't bother any longer.

As things are happening dynamically and it is best when the person is watching this, he remains in a favorable position as he knows the laws. If he is in the side of natural law, he will be in a favorable position. But going beyond the good mode, just by watching he will touch the neutral state or zero state or an undefined state which is beyond the nature of material things.

Concept 15 - Two major stumbling blocks on the path of perfection.

When the mind is focused on anything, then it leads to attachment. For becoming enlightened the mind needs to be loosened and defocused.

1. Attachment

When you are attached to your ambition, or your love interest, you become so focused that you can become attached.

You can be attached to various things it could be also sex, it could be your passion, it could be money, it could be luxuries. All these things create a barrier for your inner self to see things. The mind creates a blockage from your clean real self which is very pure. Unless you are unattached the mind is not natural, and you won't be able to see your real self.

2.Aversion - A strong dislike

Same is the case when your mind becomes focused again when you have some strong opinion or a dislike (aversion) on something.

A strong dislike can be of anything. It could be for religions other than what you are following, Certain principles which you don't agree with, certain people who are against you.

These strong views make you shift in a direction other than towards your true self.

So, these 2 things Attachment and aversion are 2 major structure blocks to enlightenment.

Concept 16 - Lust is the origin of problem or sin

Lust is something a human is fascinated to try, something different beyond the boundaries in a society.

From our childhood, some things are taboo or like we cannot be naked. Doing certain things like toilet activities are done secretly. Suddenly, when we grow up, naturally there is an urge to experiment with things which are taboo.

You will be surprised to know that things which we don't reveal to people or keep secret are the very things which lay the foundation of lust. There is always an urge for the mind to release tension. And sex is the best form of activity where the mind is released from being tensed.

If you notice sex creates a tension or takes you on a high and then releases. Unless there is tension there cannot be an equally opposite release.

Lust is something you want to satisfy yourself. It is a fantasy which mostly you think only you have. You think your fantasy is unique and want to be creative with it. Although it is exactly the same fantasy in all human beings. Because by nature or biologically more or less you are the same.

Also, lust once fulfilled it rests for some time, it again becomes active as the mind keeps on changing and it is never constant, it will always try different combinations. And these combinations are unlimited.

Lust keeps yourself covered from your real self as you will always think the satisfaction of lust is ultimate bliss. But those who have known the true self knows that the immortal self which cannot be easily explained in words is the ultimate bliss.

Once a person knows about the ultimate bliss lust becomes secondary. But to know the ultimate bliss one needs to go beyond lust and see the vanity of all the activities which a person does.

Concept 17 - How to master lust

We have 5 senses by our various organs. The senses are superior to the organs.

The mind which is where these senses get activated is superior.

The various calculations or our intellect is superior to the mind.

And the self which is hidden is superior to the intellect.

To control lust is to observe it neutrally.

One needs to understand how the senses, the organs and mind create a fantasy of lust.

It is not our real self, but a mere combination of nature inside the mind which creates a desire and fantasy. Once we see it clearly automatically lust becomes controlled or it won't harm you or you won't do the wrong things or sin. Once you start seeing clearly you will have everything under your control.

Concept 18 - Different types of practices which religion does

The majority of people are not at all aware that there is something like being enlightened.

Enlightenment is an end goal which has to be reached. All the great people who have created big religion like Jesus, Christ, Buddha, Krishna, etc. have tried to tell the secret which people have not understood, because these things cannot be learned from books, it has to be realized. It has to be experienced. It is a state.

The unenlightened priest doesn't know this. He cannot explain it as he himself doesn't know. They misguide the mass average people of low intellect.

He can only explain all the rituals which an average person adopts, thinking this the best that is possible.

People actually don't want to be enlightened, because they don't know what it is. They want that thing which they know or see. They may want wealth, they may want a beautiful wife, husband or girlfriend or boyfriend. They may want good health, fame etc. All these things can be seen. Enlightenment cannot be seen.

Now people do rituals which will fulfill all these material desires. Now there are different types of deities who they think will fulfill their specific desire. There could be one deity for health and some other deity for money. People don't really know if their wishes will get fulfilled. They do it as they think maybe it works. There is no surety what that it you do a ritual it will work. But they do it thinking at least there is no harm,

Some even do rituals because they have a fear of God. They think if they don't do the ritual, God will punish them. What kind of fear is this or slavery where one has to beg for what they want.

Some others say if you ask and then you will receive. Yes, when you have intention for something, nature takes notice and also you work towards it and it may happen.

But there are so many combinations of things that you are never sure it will happen.

Nature is so dynamic that you can be never be sure of a formula which will work.

Some do prayers, some do the mantras. Some do Pujas. Some do breathing exercises. Some give to charity.

All these things even if it is achieved it is all temporary. And again, you will lose and again you work for it or do rituals to please a deity.

Instead, find out that thing which is eternal and never changes and whereby you will achieve being in perfect bliss.

Once a person goes beyond these ritualistic practices, he really matures and finds the truth.

All rituals are bondage towards the materialistic nature.

People are confused, they say they are doing a good thing by worshipping God. But they don't understand that they are getting into the bondage.

There is no release. Know the truth by observing, being fearless to ask questions and one day you will realize the truth.

Concept 19 - Self-realized master will teach you

It will help if you listen to the audios, read books, see YouTube videos etc. But being in touch with an enlightened master will touch you and he can guide you quickly to make you enlightened.

Being with such a master. Ask the master in a humble manner. Give him your full trust and give yourself to such a master and slowly the master's enlightenment will pour into you.

Concept 20 - Is doing rituals better than acquiring transcendental knowledge.

Rituals are mere ways where you can get material desires fulfilled. Again, material desires are temporary.

Why waste time getting the temporary. Instead, acquire the knowledge which will help you see through the trap of material desire. With the transcendental knowledge you will be able to see the entire creations through yourself. Even if you have done the worst of wrong deeds, the transcendental knowledge will burn all your past wrong deeds and will take you to a new state.

Rituals cannot purify you the way acquiring transcendental knowledge will do.

Concept 21 - You are not the doer

The enlightened person realizes that what he thinks he is doing is actually a mere combination of elements of nature, which he becomes separate when he realizes enlightenment.

When a person is born, a certain number of traits are there in him, which dominates him throughout his life.

He gets the trait because of his past life deeds.

Now, whatever a person does, is primarily from these traits he has and plus the environment he interacts with.

There are different combinations of the environment and different traits which a person has. These traits in a person make a person push towards a certain behavior. And he is moved by these traits unconsciously. One needs to observe oneself of why we behave in a certain manner. You may take pride that you are a beautiful female or an intelligent, smart man, a successful man, but it's not you, it's the forces of nature inside you which are at work. Once we know and observe this then we can go beyond the mind and the inner conscious can be reached or recognized or become enlightened.

Concept 22 - The transcendental self cannot take responsibility

The spirit inside or the thing that cannot be explained easily or the real self which cannot be destroyed cannot take any responsibility as merely it is watching the different combinations of nature. Nature's combination of things actually gives a feeling of things are dynamic.

If you notice a person, there are basic traits which are always the same and when it interacts with the environment, the behavior is very much predictable if you observe minutely.

Observe yourself when you are doing things is it because you are doing or because it is there in your brain pre-programmed. Just watch your every activity closely and you will realize you are actually not doing anything but it's happening automatically. And it applies to all the bad things as well as good things.

Concept 23 - After becoming enlightened do people take birth?

After enlightenment and after death, whether the person is born again or not.

This is a strange question where we have not seen a person who has become enlightening comes back and tell that there is no birth.

How is that possible.

If he comes back and tells then he has to take birth and if he takes birth, then all the idea of rebirth becomes untrue after enlightenment.

There are lots of books which say that rebirth will not happen after burning the self.

If that is the case, then why enlightened people or deities or messiahs of great religions don't dissolve in the universe if we assume they exist.

Either they are not enlightened or its untrue that rebirth does not happen.

Also, Material Nature and self (the invisible self) go hand in hand. Without each other there seems to be no entity or movement.

Also, there is a question that why existence did create unenlightenment people and then they become enlightened. Was there any need or it is all just how the universe or existence works.

If it is that way, then it will remain that way.

There will always be a non-changing true self and changing material nature.

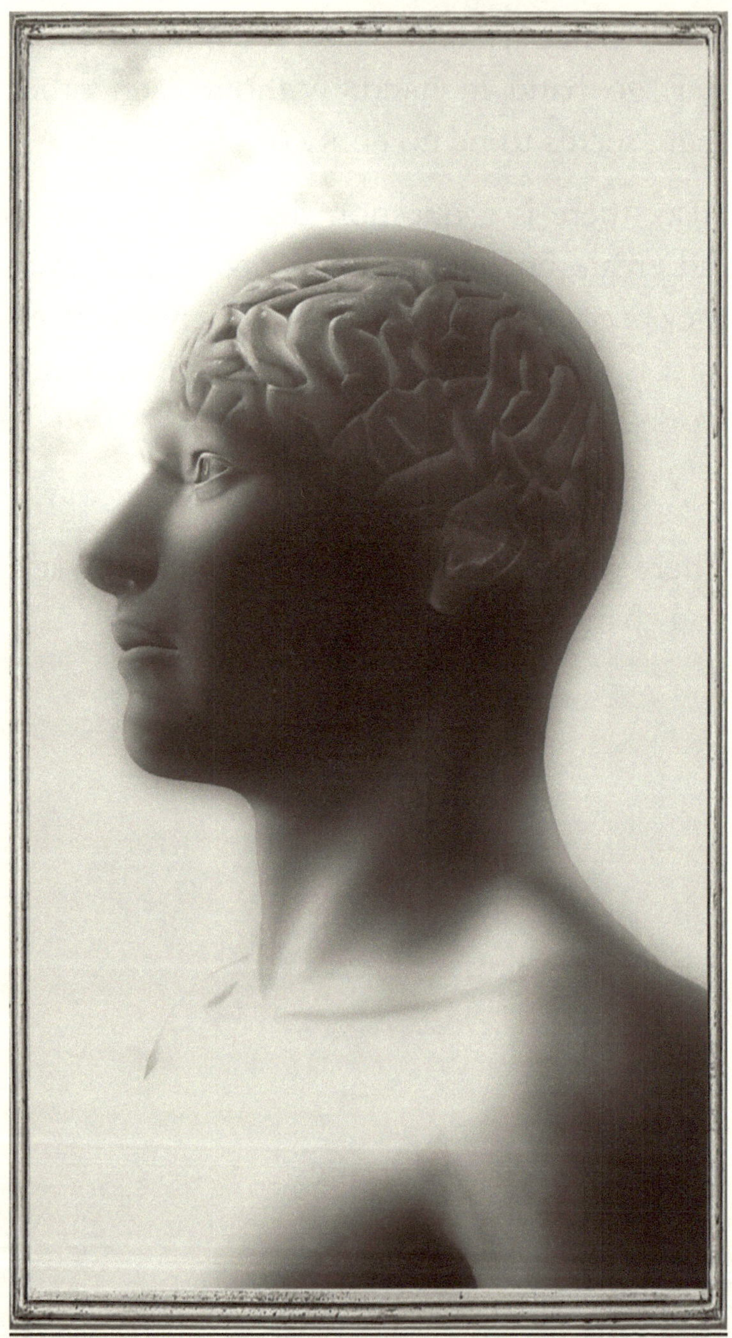

Concept 24 - Mind is the best friend as well as the worst enemy

The mind is a combination of various elements of material nature.

It is very subtle. It depends on past data to make decisions.

The mind cannot know the spirit as its very nature is material. Its inferior to the spirit

It is just a combination that is connected to the body.

And the body desires a certain comfort, and luxury.

A person who is controlled by the mind, who cannot see anything more than what the mind shows, goes towards only fulfilling his material desire.

There is chaos after some time, because material things by its very nature are perishable.

And you have to keep on putting effort to sustain it or grow it. And the mind has this thing to make its identity or ego bigger and bigger.

There is no end to it. A person will keep on running and there is only fatigue.

But if the person uses his mind to understand oneself and know the truth, the various combinations of nature.

He not only knows his immortal self, but the person is a better person in the real world also.

And the decision taken in the real world becomes more in tune with the laws of nature which favor him rather than going against him.

Concept 25 - Self-knowledge can burn all bondage of previous past doings

Your past deeds in this life or your past lives effects your traits and different facilities which you get in this life. There can be good as well as bad things you may get in this life.

How do you neutralize the bad effects of your past deeds. Is it by doing good deeds or is there a way where all your past bad effects get destroyed.

It's just by knowing yourself it gets destroyed. It gets destroyed because you are no longer affected by what happens to you by your past deed's effects.

You are in balance no matter what.

You just watch what is happening. Just like you are watching a movie. In the movie there are good and bad things. You are just watching and not getting involved with it.

 # Concept 26 - Marks of an enlightened person

An enlightened person comes to know the light within and the immortality within.

Once he realizes he comes to know that the same power is there in all beings and is driven by the power which seems endless.

The enlightened person knows the power or life inside an ant, a tree, a plant, a bird or anything. It is the same power and is the life force.

He can see but living being cannot see as they are in deep sleep. Driven more by the mind of whatever form they are in.

Everything seems to have been achieved by the enlightened person once he knows the origin of oneself. An Enlightened person comes to know that he just exists, there seems to be no beginning and end of it. As such the true unseen self seems perfect as it doesn't have any shape, it cannot be smelled, it cannot be touched, it cannot be seen or tasted or heard.

It is there but not seen.

It is diametrically opposite to the body which is seen, which can be smelled, can be touched, can be tasted and heard.

The body can be compared to another body.

The mind can be compared to another mind.

But the self is incomparable.

Body and mind's desires are all perishable.

Effort to maintain the body and mind seems to always increasing.

Looking at this the self just watches and remains aloof of all the things happening.

One becomes indifferent about the different things happening to the body and mind and the person remains stable.

Such a person is satisfied in the self itself and is not unattached to the sensual pleasures. Uncontrolled Sensual pleasures are the reasons for the misery and once that is mastered or observed from a distance, the mind is at peace.

 **Concept 27 - Sins are destroyed only by self-knowledge**

People say that if you do bad, then if you equally good things, then the bad things or sins are destroyed.

But a being has lived a lot of lives and cannot really know how much good deeds need to be done to neutralize the bad deeds.

It seems to be impossible to calculate how much bad things are done previously by us. As we cannot see our past lives. Nature has blocked all our past lives deeds on reasons why we are at particular state or stage of development.

But once we start realizing our real self, we see all the things in a neutral manner.

Immediately all the karmic deeds starts to disappear and a new positivity happens and they start reflecting on their real self while handling to others.

They are free from lust and angers effects. Means it doesn't mean they won't have lust and anger, they may still have lust and anger. But by watching the lust and anger, how it develops, they are not controlled by the ill effects of lust and anger. They let the mind to de focus and lessen the bad effects of focusing the mind into lust and anger.

Concept 28 - The ultimate knowledge

How many people strive for self-realization? Out of thousands of people, one person strives for perfection. Out of that only few put effort. Out of that barely one of them is successful.

Barely some people actually look for self-realization or enlightenment, who have already experienced the vanity of putting effort in material things of which there is no end. After a lot of effort in past lives, they now want to seek something stable and peaceful.

Yet even those people are easily disturbed by the mind.

Only a person who watches the mind can really subdue it. Any effort to subdue doesn't work.

Any technique to subdue can be used initially to train the mind, but unless a person watches oneself it won't work.

One needs to minutely observe oneself why they are doing a certain thing from its very root. It will seem difficult to observe everything.

One should ask why I am doing this, what are the factors that contribute it.

And the factors can include basic born traits, past experiences, environmental factors like people, planetary vibrations, ego, ambition, etc.

Concept 29 -Matter, consciousness and ego

We can divide the material energy into 8 parts

Likely

- The mind
- Intellect
- Ego
- Ether
- Air
- Fire
- Water
- Earth

A combination of ether, fire, water, air and earth gives you the material things which your body is made of. The body is driven by mind, intellect and ego. Behind Mind, intellect and ego is the eternal self.

Mind is a combination of past memory plus some basic born traits of the mind of a specific entity with different situations encountered by the living entity.

Intellect is a conclusion derived from the mind after going through all past data in the brain and its basic traits.

Ego is the identity of "I" created by the person, which is imaginary and again a combination of past experiences.

Concept 30 - How living being exists

There are 2 energies. One is the supreme self or supreme undefinable entity from which the material energy exists. The supreme self-combining with the material energy makes a living being. The supreme self is same in every living being but the material energy is different in different living being.

And that's the reason why there are different species and even in the same species there are infinite variation and because the material energy is not in the same capacity in different beings even in the same species.

Concept 31 - Supreme spirit is the basis of everything

The supreme spirit inside us is the taste of water. It is the radiance of the sun. It is the heat of the fire.

The 3 modes of nature in the mind namely are goodness, passion and ignorance also come from the supreme. The supreme being is not dependent on the material nature, but the material nature is dependent on the supreme being or spirit. The 3 modes of nature are so powerful that humans don't go beyond the 3 modes of nature. Going beyond the modes of nature is actually going beyond the ego, which creates a sense of I or Individuality. Going beyond the modes of nature is actually going beyond your personality.

As soon as the individuality is lost the supreme spirit is seen.

Concept 32 - How to overcome the delusive power of nature

The mind is made up of three modes of nature: goodness, passion and ignorance. It can be overcome by watching it and not getting involved in it. When you watch your mind dissolves. You dissolve just like salt dissolves in water. You have to just watch and you will touch the supreme self this very moment. Again, the mind may get bored when you do this as the mind's very nature is to move, it avoids being stable, still the very nature of self is stable and yet very dynamic.

 **Concept 33 - What is the difference between worshiping a deity and supreme self or spirit.**

People worship different deities as there are so many religions and so many different varieties of Gods.

The wishes asked by the worshiper are actually granted or happen automatically with different combinations and permutations because of the supreme spirit. And these worshippers worship generally for material gains only, as they are still controlled by the 3 modes of nature which makes a person's ego. They want to make themselves bigger and bigger. They want the 'I' in them to be shown larger in society.

Such gains by these unintelligent people who are swayed by the 3 modes of nature do not go to the supreme self or spirit. In fact, people don't really seriously seek material desires who know the supreme self, who actually sees the supreme spirit.

The people who want to know the supreme spirit or who want to become enlightened are tired of old age, the repeated cycle of birth and death, seek something beyond material nature; they want something stable and peaceful. They then seek the refuge of the supreme spirit or undefined spirit.

These people of unselfish deeds become free from the delusion of pairs of opposites of good and bad, like and dislike and start following the supreme self and become enlightened.

Concept 34 - Supreme being is not revealed to the ignorant

The Supreme being or soul is revealed to only those who seriously want to know it. And a person only wants it if they want something more than the material things. Such people are the people who are seekers of knowledge. The tired ones who had enough of this world. The distressed who want peace. These pure enquirers ultimately start knowing the supreme.

Other people are ignorant of getting fooled by nature again and again. Only those who observe the vanity of material world will want to know the supreme spirit.

Concept 35 - Everything in this creation is cyclic

The duration of creation of material living things lasts 4.32 billion years and it also gets destroyed in another 4.32 billion years. All manifestation comes from the primary material nature during these 4.32 billion years and also slowly goes back to the primary material nature during the destructive cycle.

The supreme being watches all this happening and also is part of it in the various living beings.

Scientists in our times have told that Roughly 5 billion years from now, the Sun will exhaust the hydrogen fuel in its core and start burning helium, forcing its transition into a red giant star. During this shift, its atmosphere will expand out to somewhere around 1 astronomical unit — the current average Earth-Sun distance. This means the Sun will gradually engulf Mercury, Venus, and likely Earth.

Concept 36 - Doers of ritualistic practices

There are a lot of people who are attached to the world and do religious ritualistic practices like Pooja, mantra, prayers etc. These people are mostly good people, but not much interested in knowing the true self or supreme being. But they do all the ritualistic practices and follow almost all rules. Such people go to a place called heaven where they enjoy sensual pleasures and when the effect of all the good things and ritualistic practice gets over, they come back to earth and continue their life. The ritualistic people who worship the deity, don't understand that the power inside the deity is again the supreme self. Instead of trying to know the supreme self they seem to be trapped to get materialistic things and keep worshiping the deity for getting their desires which seems to be granted by the deities but is given by the supreme self or spirit. All deities are powered by supreme self or spirit Those who know the truth, know the supreme. Although the supreme being is everywhere, it is just an illusion that there are separate entities.

 **Concept 37 - Planets and deities which control a particular cause and effect**

You must have heard that the movements of the planets affect the behavior and destiny of a particular human being or entity which can also be learned by learning astrology.

All the planets are a manifestation of the supreme being or self. The planets don't know this, but the supreme being knows this. Even if there are Gods for rain, Gods of creation, Gods of destruction, Gods of wealth and many more all these are a manifestation of the supreme soul.

All qualities like discrimination, self-knowledge, non-delusion, forgiveness, truthfulness, pleasure, pain, birth, death, fear, fearfulness, nonviolence, equanimity, prosperity, charity, fame, ill-famed, are all created by the supreme form. Great enlightened sages are born from the supreme energy. The supreme self or being is the origin of all and you are no different. You are the same, but you need to recognize it.

Concept 38 - Supreme self is both eternal as well as temporal

Supreme spirit or self consists of everything. It is inside each one of us, it is also the material nature, it is everything. There is a mask created by the material energy which gives the feeling of a different living entity.

When the mask is removed or understood, we find the same energy everywhere. The material energy is ever changing but the eternal energy is unchanging and always watching. Being powerful and not powerful comes when there is comparison.

Here there is no comparison as everything is that. Comparison comes when there is ego. If there is no individual ego where is the comparison and there is no two living beings, everything is one.

Concept 39 - Difficult to focus on the impersonal form

People don't know the impersonal, unmanifest, and formless absolute supreme soul. Because to visualize or to comprehend the unmanifest is difficult as the mind is only able to see in shapes, sound, smell, touch. That's the reason why people require a deity in front of them whereby they can see and relate.

The supreme power cannot only be confined to a deity. But if you cannot know the supreme self then at least you can use a deity, but with practice you can still focus on the unmanifest because that is the real form. The formless is the real.

Concept 40 - Ways towards becoming enlightened

There are different ways which can help you to become enlightened.

1. By getting transcendental knowledge of scriptures
2. There are mediation techniques.
3. Leaving selfish attachment to the fruits of the world.

But any one technique used, automatically the other technique is also achieved.

It is not that if one method is used, then other method's effect is not achieved. You will still know the other method. Based on a person's strength or weakness one may prefer a particular method.

Part 2

 **Concept 41 - Attributes of a person of being enlightened or devotee of being enlightened.**

One who does not have any greed has understood the dual modes of nature of likes and dislike.

Who is friendly and compassionate.

Free from the notion of I and my who is ever content and subdued by his mind.

Whose resolve is firm and mind and intellect is towards the supreme self or spirit

Concept 42 - Creation is the creator

Creation is the creator, those who understand this statement verily knows the truth.

People think that there is a person or a God, who has created the world. That is not the truth, the truth is that creation and creator are the same.

In the sense the painter and painting are same. The painter is not separate from the painting.

To create the creation without the creator getting involved in the creation is not possible. Because all the things living and nonliving are part of the creation and creator.

You and we are the part of the creation. It is only because of the mind we think we are different from the creator.

We get an identity only because of the different modes of nature and its combination. We assume there is a creator because we cannot imagine that how the world is created by its own. And we cannot imagine that the creator is also here as, without the power of the creator nothing can move. It is also because of the creator inside the creation, things are happening. And its delusive force (Maya) doesn't let us know the truth unless after a lot of time of sheer exhaustion of the cyclic world a person tries to know it.

It is the mind which realizes or moves towards enlightenment, because the eternal self is already realized. The entity or mind realizes it. The mind one realized remains in the self. At this point the true self sees through and through, but here it has gone beyond the mind.

To a certain extent only mind can be used to go towards enlightenment. Later, even the mind needs to be dropped.

Concept 43 - Qualities which leads to enlightenment

1. Humility
2. Modesty
3. Non-Violence
4. Forgiveness
5. Honesty
6. Service to guru
7. Purity of thoughts
8. Steadfastness
9. Self-control
10. Aversion to sense objects
11. Absence of ego
12. Constant reflection on pain and suffering
13. Indifferent in birth, death, old age, disease and death

These are some qualities which can lead to enlightenment. Because the mind gets trained and starts thinking. These are qualities either you have it and then get enlightenment, or you become enlightened and then get it.

Generally, an average person needs to get the qualities and then it leads to enlightenment.

 **Concept 44 - Means to Nirvana**

1. Detachments
2. Non fondness with son, wife, and home
3. Unfailing equanimity upon attainment of the desirable and the undesirable.
4. Devotion to the supreme self or spirit
5. Taste for solitude
6. Distaste for social gathering and gossip
7. Steadfastness in acquiring the knowledge of spirit
8. Seeing the only presence of spirit everywhere.

This is knowledge contrary to this is ignorance.

Concept 45 - That which cannot be perceived and explained

The superior self or your purest self is watching over the material nature as it gets divided into three modes of nature

1. • Goodness
2. • Passion
3. • Ignorance

It watches over the material nature without being attached. But it also drives the material nature based on its laws and traits. The behavior of material nature seems little difficult to predict as its diametrically opposite to the watching supreme spirit. In both the places the supreme spirit is there.

A combination of spirit and body with mind makes an entity. An entity which is imaginary yet looks so true. In fact, everything that happens is actually inside the spirit. If the spirit doesn't see the material nature. There won't be any material nature. Spirit is inside as well as outside of all beings.

Although the spirit is nearest to you than anything else, but for the ignorant it is very far. For the ignorant it is undivided and appears divided.

People think of God as the creator, sustainer and destroyer. But all are the same. In fact, it is the material nature which seems to divide the supreme into different gods. But without the power of the supreme nothing can move. He is to be realized by self- knowledge only.

Having understood this the devotee or genuine seeker attains the supreme.

Concept 46 - Begin less spiritual and material nature

People can believe that the spirit is eternal. They want to believe it, although they don't know how it is possible. They think of themselves as people who are bound to die with innumerable limitations and diseases. They worship a god who they think doesn't have all these limitations.

But what people fail to believe is that just as the spirit is begin less, the material nature is also begin less and if it is begin less, it is also endless.

People's notation to go towards the spirit and ignore the material energy is wrong. As both exist together of course to know the spirit, one needs to go beyond the material nature. Knowing the spirit one cannot ignore the material nature.

Concept 47 - How the body is evolved

All manifestations of living beings are because of three modes of nature, namely goodness, passion and ignorance.

Material nature is said to be the cause of production of physical body and organs of perception and action.

Based on the subtle nature of the mind a living being is born. The combination of which is difficult to comprehend.

Based on past lives deeds or karmas of living being a particular birth is possible in a different womb. Karmic deeds (Deeds of past life) are the cause of birth.

State of mind you are in is very important during death. If you have a stable mind in the mode of goodness, then you will get a body in next life similarly.

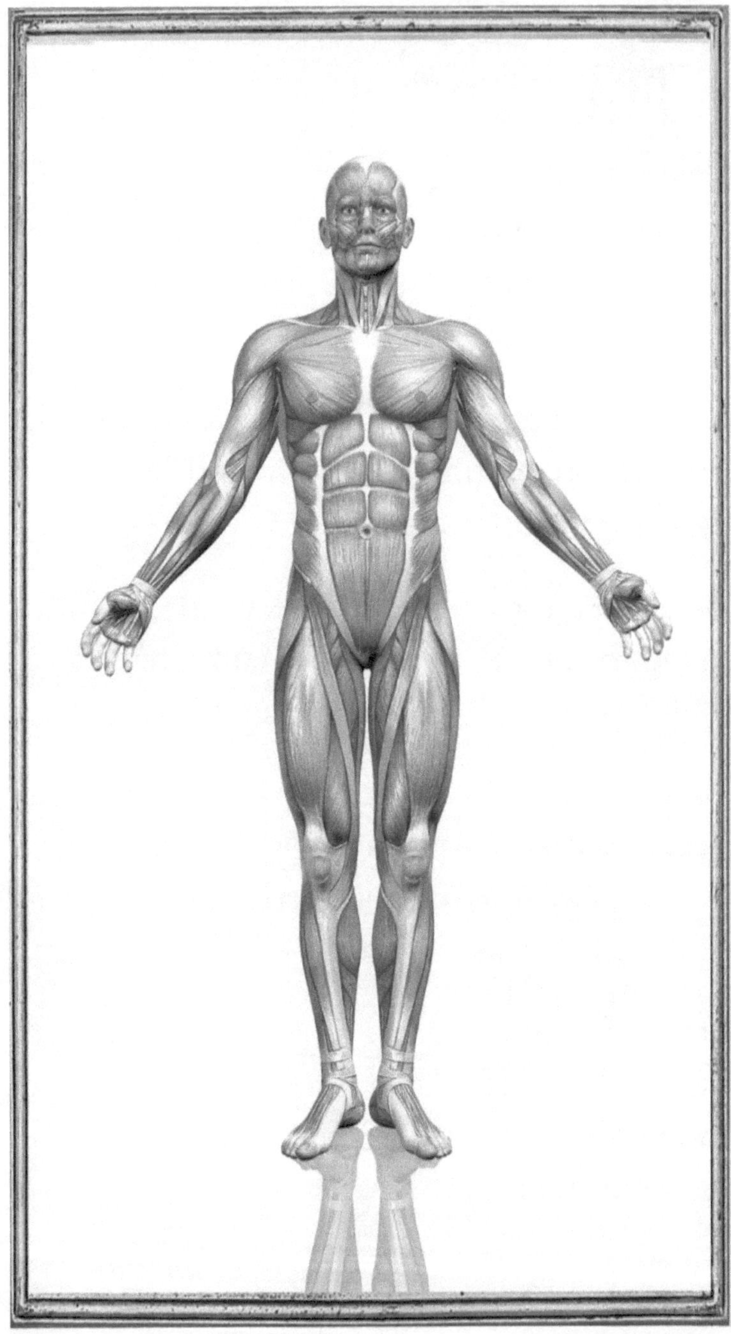

Concept 48 - The great witness

The spirit in the body is a witness. It is a witness to all the things in the body. It is a witness of the eyes, which sees the world. It is a witness to what we hear. It is a witness of what we smell. It is a witness of what we touch. It is a witness of our memory. It is a witness of the various combinations and calculations of what we do.

When we ourselves become a witness of all the things we do, we are one with the supreme soul.

Concept 49 - The supreme soul is the great supporter

Have you seen dead bodies without any movement? The dead body is without movement because the supreme soul is absent or ceases to exist in the body. And hence without the support the body ceases to exist. Unless the person in his life reaches the supreme witness state, the entity keeps on taking repeated births entangled without complete freedom, until a perfection is reached. The person keeps evolving towards enlightenment. The supreme spirit wants peace for everyone, but unless the mind of the person decides to take it and go towards the path it won't happen. The supreme spirit also cannot force things to happen unless an entity decides to allow it. An entity is limited by his past experiences and may not have complete knowledge compared to what the supreme spirit has.

Hence, it's better to surrender or dissolve oneself and suddenly the magic or enlightenment happens. Suddenly you are in the right direction.

The person has to jump into knowing the supreme soul or spirit, because by calculation you may never decide to become enlightened.

Concept 50 - Supreme spirit is the enjoyer and controller

You must be thinking that you are enjoying when you have sex or any other kind of activity. But it's the mind which enjoys and gives an impression of enjoyment. But beyond the mind the enjoyer and controller is the supreme spirit.

The supreme spirit is actually behind everything without which there is no perception.

Again, enjoyment is something which is created and hence its imaginary (Maya). But even the imaginary is experienced by the supreme spirit only.

Concept 51 - Supreme spirit is the controller

Have you noticed that sometimes you miss getting into an accident or if you had taken a step there could have been an accident. But that doesn't happen.

There is a something inside you that controls you from doing it. It is none but the supreme spirit who knows better than you and didn't allow you to do it.

The supreme spirit is the controller in you and it decides on what has to be done.

Imagine how this world is so systematically working. How is it possible without a set of rules and combination and a controller.

Concept 52 - How is the supreme spirit realized

The supreme spirit can be realized by meditation or by observing or by understanding metaphysical knowledge which will lead to the supreme spirit. If one method is followed automatically you can also know the other.

There are various meditation techniques. All techniques train you to observe your mind and body. And when you observe you do the same thing as the supreme being is doing and you are one with it.

By learning metaphysical knowledge from books, videos, audios, you can understand. But you need to realize within. This can come only by putting an effort to realize. After some time, you may get tired that enlightenment is not happening to you will give up the effort when you give up the effort something incredible you will realize. When the pressures of the mind are released. When the mind becomes inactive or you go beyond your mind, that thing which cannot be described happens.

 **Concept 53 - All living beings are born from union of spirit and matter**

All beings are born from the union of spirit and matter. Matter is dead without the spirit.

The brain is dead without the life of the spirit.

You feel alive is because of the spirit. But you think of yourself as the body. Because the spirit sees from the body. You assume the qualities of body and mind because the mind creates an illusion.

The one who knows this also knows that the eternal spirit is equally there in all beings.

Concept 54 - You won't hurt your own self

The one who sees the same eternal supreme spirit dwelling as spirit equally within all mortal beings can really see.

When one sees the self in all living beings a big compassion arises for the unknowing living being. Because the same self is everywhere and you cannot feel like hurting them. Knowing this, one attains the supreme

Concept 55 - Powers of material nature

One who perceives that all works are done by the powers of material nature truly understands. Diverse variety of living beings are formed by the material nature, but that is supported from spirit alone. In Fact, the personality of a person is basically a combination of material nature in varied quantities.

Fools thinks it's their personality, but it is actually just a mere combination of things which they are forced to use.

They are always trying to get the right varied quantity of material nature to be successful in material life. For that they pray and do various rituals, but they don't know that to go beyond material nature is where the ultimate bliss is. They have a notation of heaven, where it is full of material things to fulfill their natural desire. It could be sex, food or positions or powers or anything.

The thing they desire now and work now, they think they will get more as a reward in heaven.

Concept 56 - The impersonal God

There are devotees who worship a form of God. But here they become divided into two. As they consider themselves and God separate. And it becomes difficult for them to think they are equal to the person whom they worship.

A devotee has the impression of being inferior and God is superior. But the worshiper and worshiped are the same.

A devotee can worship the personal form of God, but unless after a certain time they merge, it will be a stumbling block to worship a particular deity.

The last block where the mind is clinging to a personal form of deity is very difficult to change, and it may take a lot of time, but ultimately, they may merge.

Concept 57 - Worshiping the impersonal form of God

Those who worship the unchangeable, the unexplainable, the invisible, the one present, the inconceivable, the unchanging, the immovable and the formless aspect of God are the closest and slowly and steadily they also merge into it.

All divisions need to be broken whether it is personal or impersonal God.

Even those who worship the unchangeable spirit, need to understand that unless all the divisions are broken you are still in the same boat as a person who is worshiping the personal form of God.

Concept 58 - The supreme is nearest to you

The supreme spirit which is closest to you, only your mind is the hindrance. There is absolutely no one closer to you than the spirit.

You are the spirit when there is no gap between you and the spirit, you are as it is watching from the body in which you reside.

Observing, enjoying, crying, having sex, watching sports, doing your duty, eating, drinking. All this is happening because of the combination of the natural elements of your body. It is a mere combination of things.

As the supreme spirit is constant in nature and diametrically opposite to the material energy. The material energy with its infinite variations keeps the spirit amused, involved and watching, like it is seeing a movie.

Concept 59 - Modes of Nature – Goodness

Goodness, passion and ignorance are the 3 modes of nature which are actually built in your mind.

You use it in varied quantities, sometimes one quantity is dominant. Sometimes it is mixed. It is difficult to understand what is happening unless you see yourself.

In the mode of Goodness a person becomes more ethical. In this mode, compassion in a person increases and they start doing things the right way and ultimately also benefit materialistically. But after some time, even in the goodness mode a person gets fed up. Because they always cannot be in the mode of goodness. Nature at times drags to be passionate or ignorant.

Once a person gets fed up of cyclic things happening, they go in search to find if there is something more.

Questions such as "who am I", "where have I come from", "Have I just got born accidentally", such questions bother them and they seek the truth.

Concept 60 - Modes of nature – Passion

Modes of passion are characterized by the fantasy created by the mind to satisfy intense sense gratification. Sense gratification triggers a lot of things to gratify your senses. For example, for attracting the opposite sex, one starts to put effort to get more material things, like money and asset which can attract the opposite sex. Hence it triggers a list of things and they remain focused on it.

These activities bind the person to its fruit. If the result is not achieved, they become miserable. Also, it has to be noted the mind generates a varied amount of mode of passion in a person and so does a person behave accordingly in a certain manner.

Concept 61 - Modes of nature – Ignorance

Mode of ignorance is the deluder which comes from sharp ego and binds the entity to carelessness, laziness and excessive sleep.

Mode of ignorance comes because of excessive thinking of "I" and not concerning about others. They see themselves as an individual and no other person is important.

Hurting others won't matter to them till the time their wishes are fulfilled.

Such a person has no idea what to do and what not to do, what is right and what is wrong. These people need to get transformed in the mode of passion and slowly, then to the mode of goodness. Then finally later they can also realize the truth, but it may take a lot of time, maybe lots of lives. Such people who have little compassion, constantly are trapped by their wrong doings and face the consequence more and more. Unless they have a deliberate attempt to change, they can fall down and tend to be born in a less good family and live a life of misery.

The Mode of goodness can also lead to happiness in the material world. But only if you go beyond the mode of goodness, then only enlightenment is possible

The mode of passion attaches to you achieving something. The activities done in the mode of passion can also be good, but it still attaches the mind because it is focused and tense.

The mode of ignorance attaches us to traps all around us, as there is a break of natural law and the individual always tends to fall in the trap in the wrong side of nature.

Concept 62 - The three modes of nature are vehicles of transmigration

It seems that when a person dies when he is in the mode of goodness seems to grow to a higher life in his next life. But it also doesn't mean he has touched the supreme spirit. Only when a person is beyond any colors of the modes of nature does one know the truth.

There seems to be a wrong perception that a person in the mode of goodness becomes enlightened. No, a person has to leave everything that is generated by material nature. And material nature generates modes of goodness. Even that has to be given up to achieve the infinite.

Concept 63 - When a person dies in the mode of passion

When a person dies in the mode of passion, they are born again to fulfill what they had desired. It is the combination of mental state which creates the body in the next life and they go on in their pursuit to fulfill their dreams.

Concept 64 - When a person dies in the mode of ignorance

When one dies in the mode of ignorance one is reborn as a lower creature then what they were.

Based on their mental state.

There are numerous stories of reincarnations if you doubt this.

Also, there are ways like hypnosis where you can have a glimpse of your past life.

But you don't have to wait for your next life. You can reach the supreme right now itself.

It is your very nature which you have forgotten because of the mind with is modes of nature.

What will happen tomorrow or in the future or in this life or next life should not matter to you.

What you can do is change now and go towards the direction. Then everything will fall in place.

 **Concept 65 - Going beyond birth, old age and death.**

So, what goes wrong with life actually, when we attach ourselves to our body and mind, then there is a problem. Because the mind by its very nature goes up and down and is never stable and if you are attached to it there is no doubt in it that you wouldn't be in peace.

Similarly, the body is always deteriorating from birth till death.

There is a disease inbuilt called old age where the cells keep deteriorating and you may have back pain, leg pain, headache, etc. there is no dearth of diseases which can make you miserable.

It can make you unstable, initially when you are young all may seem fine, but what happens when disease or old age comes, all the enjoyment seems to become a torture.

Hence there is a need for you to discover the thing without disease, which is everlasting, which is always peaceful.

Concept 66 - A combination of matter

When you see a person, it could be seen that if you observe very carefully, they actually don't exist. What exists is the watcher and a combination of matter in a raw form and in a subtle form.

A living entity is moving the body, deciding on the actions.

A baby born learns to do that, but a learned adult is also in its own limitations. We think we are deciding to do things, but things happen automatically with its various combinations.

There seems to be life in a body, but it is not life only in a body. Life is everywhere, spirit is everywhere, it is just that a part of material nature that takes itself as separate and starts thinking oneself as different.

Concept 67 - Qualities to develop that leads to enlightenment

1. Fearlessness
2. Purity
3. Trying to know about self-knowledge
4. Charity
5. Sense restraint
6. Sacrifice
7. Study of the scriptures

These are qualities which leads to enlightenment. I am not explaining them in great detail, but as you can see and meditate on it. It's very much self-explanatory.

Concept 68 - Qualities which should be given up for spiritual journey

Hypocrisy – When a person is afraid of the consequences of doing the right things, they try to be like a politician who can change depending on a situation not knowing that ultimately the laws of nature has its own way.

Arrogance - Arrogance is born out of a desire to be recognized. It is an extreme behavior of a person who is not recognized and starts putting effort so that he becomes recognized.

And at a later stage just to show his superiority to convince oneself and others, behave in a manner which looks very aggressive and its productive effect is very short lived.

Everything is bound by the forces of nature. Sooner or later nature is a great leveler.

One needs to understand things in which your mind becomes focused and things where your mind becomes defocused or released. When there is a release, then it leads to growth and when there is tension, it leads you lower.

Just relax and in relaxation all decisions are devoid of any arrogance and pride.

 ## Concept 69 - Anger, harshness and ignorance

Anger comes when a particular desire is not fulfilled or a person thinks that the desire had to be fulfilled but didn't get fulfilled.

Anger is also like a defense mechanism where a person becomes so aggressive to protect himself and his identity. To lose anger is to lose one's identity. By losing one's identity one goes beyond the 3 modes of nature.

When you get angry, just release and give up and see immediately you are moving towards nothingness.

Concept 70 - The world is for sex and nothing else for the disillusioned

The people who are disillusioned, think that only sex matter and nothing else. They may think the union of men and women alone causes the world.

These people with endless anxiety lasting until death consider sense gratification as their highest aim, convinced that sense pleasure is everything.

Bewildered by many fantasies, entangled in the net of delusion, addicted to the enjoyment of sensual pleasures they fall down.

Once a person becomes enlightened, the sexuality in a person decreases or becomes nil. But they do have sex just as a person eats, walks, defecates. As sex is a natural thing. Only by being attached to sexuality it becomes a problem. Once the sexuality disappears, then the person is in the right direction. The point is whatever happens to the mind and body should be like a dream, but you also know that in reality or in your original state, there was nothing.

Concept 71 - As you can go higher you can also go lower and lower

The spirit inside everyone wants you to attain the spirit. God seeks you more than man seeks God. But the cruel, hater, sinful people keep going into the material world to enjoy material nature. Nothing wrong enjoying the material world. But thinking that is all and ignoring to know the true self which is more blissful, there lies the problem. One keeps on going towards the gross or raw things instead of going towards more subtle things.

Really, there is something which is better than the cyclic material world, its full of peace and there is nothing more required. But people can only see what they can see in the material world and aggressively try to get it by any means without any compassion for other people.

Concept 72 - The gates of hell, lust, anger, greed

You have got the perception of hell either from religious books or people talking about, whether it exists or not you need to really understand it and how it affects you. Hell is something which you won't like or something where you are tortured. Torture in the physical and mental sense. Hell can be here, or it can be anywhere. Basically, hell may be physical and mental torture.

Ignorance causes a living entity to go below more and more to lower levels.

The spirit is observing all this but would always like to relieve you of the pains. There is nothing the spirit does or can do unless the living entity ask for it.

It depends on the living entity to ask, when you ask, things start happening. But what, you ask may be good or bad for you which you may assume it may be always be good.

The world has qualities good and bad. Those are qualities will lead to growth or no growth.

Existence follows laws and you need to recognize and choose what laws are good for you.

Concept 73 - Scriptures as authority

Man has enough intelligence to find out the truth, but due to his attachment to the material things he is unable to do it.

In a confused state a person who seeks answers to unanswered questions, at such a situation which is normally the situation of all, he should take the assistance of the scriptures given by enlightened people excluding any ritualistic procedures, doing it he moves towards the supreme being.

There are a lot of books you can refer ranging from Bhagavat Gita, Upanishads, Buddhism, Bible, Books of Great Master like Osho, Zen, J.Krishnamurthy etc. or any master famous or not famous who acts as a guide.

Concept 74 - Duties and modes of native whom you worship

People in the mode of Goodness or a little bit in the mood of goodness worship Gods, deities or enlightened masters of a particular type which leads them.

Those in the mode of passion may worship deities of a particular type lower than the mode of goodness which leads them.

Those in the mode of ignorance may worship deities of a particular type lower than the mode of passion which leads them.

A deity or the person they follow will reflect a particular dominant quality in their behavior. People following a particular deity may also take only those qualities from the deities of which they worship.

But it is always not necessary that those who worship a particular deity may be fully ignorant or passionate or good.

They can be partially good, ignorant or passionate.

A particular deity may be having all modes, but the devotee may choose only a particular quality based on their developmental stage.

I have seen based on their nature, a particular, a person only sees a particular quality in the deity.

Although it may be that a particular deity may have all the qualities.

Those who look at the formless nature of God really, they are the one who reach to the divine.

All other forms see a consolidation to weak minds who are not able to go beyond a certain thinking.

Concept 75 - Can a person who is enlightened be affected by having sex.

There is a wrong view that if you have sex enlightenment will be affected.

Once a person realizes his enlightenment nothing can change it.

He will be in bliss and nothing can change it.

Sex becomes mere a thing like you eat, drink, urinate, etc., it becomes a biological thing.

Enlightenment does not mean that you don't do your bodily things.

You can do sex, but enlightenment is not affected by it. It does not depend on the body.

Once the mind is cleared of the dust, it can remain as it is.

Concept 76 - Can a person remain enlightened and also be ambitious.

Just like the air is all around, so is the enlightened person all around and sees all objects without being affected.

So, a person can be enlightened and still live his day-to-day life with all its colors just like a normal person is living.

Obviously, when a person is living, the body has its requirements and sometimes it can also require some comfort which can be ambitious. But it will never go out of hand as the enlightened person knows the laws of nature and knows what is right and wrong.

So, any decisions by an enlightened person will always be for good.

By observing and seeing that everything repeats in a cyclic manner the enlightened person becomes indifferent to it.

Concept 77 - Know a person by the food they eat.

Well, there are basically 3 types of food.

Foods that promote virtue, strength, health, happiness, joy, Longevity like fruits, vegetables, juices, dry fruits are juicy, smoothing and nutritious. People in the mode of goodness like such foods. And knows what is right and wrong.

So, the decisions will always be for good.

Seeing that everything repeats is a cyclic manner. The enlightenment becomes indifferent to it.

b) Foods that are very bitter, sour, salty, pungent, dry and burning, which cause pain, grief and disease. Excess of salty, pungent food like chips, soup, chicken meat, alcohol. They are liked by people in the mode of passion.

c) The foods liked by people in the mode of ignorance are stale, tasteless, not juicy, rotten and impure foods kept stale for days, not properly cooked food etc.

Based on these indicators you can now which modes of nature is dominant in you and you can work on it.

Concept 78 - Types of work or service

When we are doing anything, observe for what you are doing it, in which mode does it come. Whether it is in the mode of goodness, passion or ignorance. Or a combination of two or three modes.

a) Service without the desire for fruit with a firm belief, conviction that it is a duty is in the mode of goodness.

Although even this type of work will get good karma or fruits later in their life journey. You can do anything like working for your society, or as a charity, just to help someone without any specific intention of getting returns. These activities are in the mode of goodness.

b) Service or work that is performed only for show and aiming for fruit, know that this is the mode of passion. Means you may want to be a star, footballer, cricketer or an actor or help someone like a politician just to show yourself as big, know that such person to be in the mode of passion.

c) Service that is performed without food being distributed or devoid of gift or compassion harming someone, know that these activities to be in the mode of ignorance.

A person may be in the mode of ignorance e like a terrorist who lives for their own selfish goals.

Knowing this, one should not get trapped in the inferior modes of nature.

If you are in the mode of ignorance or ,passion then a move towards mode of goodness and later e even go beyond mode of goodness and attain enlightenment.

 **Concept 79 - Austerity of deed**

The worship of celestial controllers, the priest, guru, the wise, purity, honesty, celibacy, and non-violence are called the austerity of deeds.

These things are required when a person is seeking enlightenment as the opposite of these things creates hindrance towards becoming enlightened.

But once a person is enlightened, all these things don't really matter.

People who are undisciplined or unenlightened give importance to those things, but who have already traveled the path, nothing really matters to them.

It doesn't mean that an enlightened person will do the things which are wrong. Automatically an enlightened person will always tend to do the right things.

Concept 80 - Infinite people and creatures which don't exist.

We can see an infinite number of creatures, ranging from insects, to worms, to animals, to birds to humans.

Everything is moving, doing some action, but those are a mere combination of matter which is powered by the invisible spirit or the unknown. In fact, the unknown spirit exists everywhere, but the mind thinks it is a separate entity and the creature thinks like a separate individual. The one spirit is alive in material nature. Actually, the spirit is the experiencer and the observed as well.

The spirit watching in all the bodies is one, but makes into infinite bodies.

It is alone, yet infinite.

It wants to be alone but also wants to be infinite.

If it did not want to be infinite, the world would not have existed yet it's still undivided, that's the paradox. That's the very nature of existence. You may tend to wonder why such an arrangement. Well, it is how existence has worked. There is no start or end to it. There is no reason to it.

Concept 81 - Austerity of speech

Speech that is non offensive, truthful, pleasant, beneficial and that is also used to study scriptures is called as austerity of word.

You may have seen people who are very non offensive, try to pacify by speaking in a manner, where they understand, there seems a lot of patience in them,

They have patience because they see others as one who is like oneself.

They have patience because they feel the love for others.

Such people, by their goodness, finally see the vanity of the world, where things go on in circles.

They finally start studying the scripture, books, videos, listen to the audios, follow the Gurus to know the truth.

Concept 82 - Austerity of thought

The serenity of mind, gentleness, equanimity, self-control and the purity of thought – these are called austerity of thought.

You may have seen people who are ignorant or passionate where they have an aggression or anger where their mind keeps running, automatically without knowing.

Such people lack gentleness or self-control in being neutral in their thoughts.

It is austerity for people who lack it, but it is not austerity for people who have it.

If you are listening to this and if you feel you lack any of the qualities then try to relax when you are thinking, don't force yourself, just let the mind relax and you will automatically become gentle and take decisions in equanimity.

Concept 83 - Combined Austerity and its results

Without a desire for fruit of work it is said to be austerity in the mode of goodness.

Because sometimes desiring the fruit can be really unpredictable. There are various combinations required for it which may or may not be in your control.

You may be born with a trait you may try to achieve contrary to it plus, you may or may not have the facilities to fulfill it.

At the most you can do is try to do the best or more than best of your abilities.

Enjoy the process and that will give more joy and then the results itself.

Concept 84 - Austerity in the mode of passion

Austerity that is performed for gaining respect, honor, reverence, and for the sake to gain temporary result is said to be in the mode of passion.

Effort when you put in to gain recognition, maybe in society, maybe in the family, maybe in politics, maybe in sports can be said to be in the mode of passion. They may gain respect, but in the process may disrespect others.

If you notice in sports or areas where there is one or more competition there seems no respect for the other opponent.

The selfish ego for a person in mode of passion always comes first. The person thinks he is always better than the other and tries to win every time without understanding whether he deserves it or not.

Or even in politics, you can see whether a person deserves it or not, and wants a post not necessary it will benefit people.

A fear is there of not getting recognized. A fear of failure to project one's own capability.

Capabilities are a combination given to an entity. He or she doesn't really own it.

Concept 85 - Austerity of ignorance

Austerity performed with foolish stubbornness or with self-torture or harming others is declared to be in the mode of ignorance.

Sometimes people take a stand just to win, just to satisfy their ego. It won't matter for them whether they are right or wrong. They just want their way and they are stubborn towards it.

They may even self-torture, which really doesn't make any sense to torture the vehicle or the body by which they function.

They may even harm others like terrorist, extreme sports people, who get into fights with no compassion for the other person and the body and they will damage, the gift that they have received to be born as a human being with infinite intelligence.

Concept 86 - Charity

a) Charity in the mode of goodness

Charity when you are doing as a duty at a right place to the deserving candidate who does not take anything in return is considered to be in the mode of goodness.

Maybe you are helping someone on the road, or in your society, office just for the sake of it not expecting anything. Without accepting anything in return, when love is the only reason, you are doing the charity, then it is termed as a charity in the mode of goodness.

b) Charity in the mode of passion

When a person gives charity so that the Gods are impressed so that in return, he will get back something in return is said to be in the mode of passion.

Politicians give charity so that they get votes.

A religious follower gives to charity because their priest insists them to do charity in the name of God and they do it thinking their desires will be fulfilled, they may give 10 Rs and then think God will fulfill their desire of crores of Rupees.

What does existence wants or sees while receiving charity is the love by which they give, is a feeling of purity by which a person gives. When there is love, the person disappears and God appears.

c) <u>Charity in the mode of ignorance</u>

Increase in passion leads to disappointment which ultimately becomes a mode of ignorance.

A person in the mode of ignorance will give charity, but will give it to an unworthy person without any rules, it will be with ridicule to the person who is receiving it.

In this utter ignorance the person keeps lower levels of existence and keep committing sins.

Concept 87 - Understanding Actions

There is a misconception that when you do or say things, then only its action.

Even when you think there is movement in action.

An action which is right or wrong is because of these 3 things: thoughts, words and deeds.

But how does one person's action differ from the other. For the ignorant person he thinks he himself is the doer or his body is doing in his ignorant views.

But it is not that way. There are mainly five causes or five combinations in various quantities which make up an action.

Namely – 1) There is a physical body which is alive with a mind.

Now the physical body varies with different people, although the basic framework is still the same.

There could be a lot of variations in a physical body maybe a short, tall, fat body or a mind which can take more calculations or a mind which cannot pass a lot of calculations or a mind which is inclined to a certain specific area. The variations can go on and on based on what the physical body and mind's variation. Based on these variation the activities differ significantly in a person when he is doing the action. The basic traits are really programmed in their body and mind.

2) The modes of nature

A person's mind is mostly in 3 modes, either in goodness mode, passion mode or ignorance mode.

Based on these modes they take decisions. So how can a person be in modes like passion and ignorance and change to the mode of goodness is by watching them.

Letting the ego relax, by simply watching what you are doing or meditating on what you are doing and automatically things will be in goodness mode. But it is difficult and it takes practice to change things, it may not happen overnight.

3) The gross organs of sense

Namely 2 hands, 2 legs, nose, ear, mouth, eye, skin.

4) Various combinations of the mind - The mind with its own trait along with various positions of the planets or vibrations influenced by planetary movement which controls various destinies, by actively reacting with the environment a person is in. Have you observed, there are times when you behave in a certain manner, maybe romantic, maybe angry, maybe foolish, maybe intellectual. This is called the pull from the vibrations created by various planetary movements.

The fifth part is something which people are not aware of or cannot believe. But if you observe closely, there are times for certain things, and it happens accordingly. These forces actually force you to bear the fruit of your past Karmas or things which has happened in this life or past lives.

These 5 things, namely make the actions of living being work

Concept 88 - Passion knowledge

People are competing against each other nowadays, they want to prove themselves, that they are better than others.

They don't feel that the other person is same as oneself. Their egos need to be satisfied so to prove themselves, they do everything to look superior, maybe in sports, activity, office, creativity or anything.

These people see everybody as separate from the others.

Such knowledge where they compete with others, to satisfy the ego is to be known as knowledge in the mode of passion.

You can see a lot of businessmen, sports persons, actors, corporate people and even general people who belong to this category.

For these people the pleasures in the beginning, which they would see like nectar later becomes poison.

Part 4

Concept 89 - Tools for enlightenment - Meditation

Although there is no specific technique for enlightenment.

There are some meditation techniques which can help

What is meditation?

Meditation is an adventure into the unknown, the greatest adventure human can take, to the complete unknown, which cannot be known, or understood. As the mind can only be a speculator and is incapable to go beyond.

Meditation is just to be, not doing anything, no action, no thought, no emotion.

In fact, you don't even try to push yourself into anything, allow what is happening, just watch, be a watchman.

You just are and being in the present is sheer delight.

Whenever you can just be, drop all doing.

Thinking is doing.

Concentration is doing.

Contemplation is doing.

Just be be the watchman

Essential core, the spirit of meditation is to actually learn how to witness.

How to experience the bliss being the witness.

Meditation means awareness. Whatsoever you do with awareness is meditation.

Walking can be a meditation if you walk alert.

Listening to the birds can be a meditation if you listen with awareness.

Think of yourself as a watching spirit who has suddenly got a body with arms, legs, ear, eyes, nose, mouth and mind.

Just listening to the inner noise of your mind can be a meditation if you remain alert and watchful.

Concept 90 - Tools for enlightenment – Vipassana Meditation

Vipassana Meditation

Vipassana Meditation is the meditation, which has actually made more enlightened people, than any other way.

Vipassana is very simple.

Even a child can do it.

There are three ways of Vipassana Meditation.

Concept 91 - Tools for enlightenment – Vipassana Meditation -Type 1

1 – Vipassana - Awareness

In the first type you need to be aware of your actions, your body, mind, your heart.

First, sit in a comfortable position be still and just move your hand. Moving your hand observe that the body is separate, and you are controlling it separately.

There seems to be 2 parts to you.

Similarly, try walking, walk with awareness, and in the center is you, which is the invisible spirit. Move body like a mechanical thing.

Be alert of the movements of your body when you are eating.

While taking a shower, be alert to the sound of water.

Just be alert.

Similarly, do it in your mind.

What thought comes to your mind. When it comes, why is there a combination of thoughts in your mind.

What emotions are coming to your mind.

Don't judge what is wrong, right, just observe, the intelligence will come automatically.

Know it do it continuously for every activity for quite some time, till you get it or realize your soul or spirit.

Concept 92 - Tools for enlightenment – 2nd type of Vipassana Meditation - Breathing

The second form of Vipassana meditation is becoming aware of breathing.

As the breath goes in, your belly starts rising up and as the breath goes out, your belly starts settling down.

So, in this method is to be aware of the belly its rising and falling.

Once you become more and more aware of the belly, the mind becomes silent, the mood disappears.

Slowly, with a silent mind, you will touch the soul and start becoming aware of the distinction between your soul, mind and body.

Concept 93 - Tools for enlightenment – 3rd Type of Vipassana Meditation

The third type of Vipassana meditation. is to be aware of the breath at the entrance, when the breath goes in through your nostrils.

Follow it till it reaches the other extreme or till the breath goes in. Feel if when it passes through the nose.

Then when the breath goes out follow it as it goes from one extreme into outside your nose.

These are one of the best forms of meditation.

Anyone can do it.

As you become used in this meditation your mind will become silent, the ego will disappear and the feeling of "I" will slowly disappear.

You will feel at bliss being at the peak of this state. The whole of you becoming completely blank or into nothingness.

The bliss that nothingness beings is incomparable.

Vipassana walks

In Vipassana walk you need to walk in a circle or in a line of 10 to 15 steps going back and forth, inside or out of doors.

Eyes should be focused on the ground few steps distance ahead.

While walking attention should be on the feet touching the ground.

It is the same technique as doing Vipassana in sitting posture. You can do it for 20 to 30 minutes.

 **Concept 94 - Tools for enlightenment – Pointing method**

This is a very easy to do exercise. Key to getting a glimpse of enlightenment experience is to simply follow the steps. Slowly and steadily repeating this exercise will help in your journey

1. Now, whether you are sitting, lying down or standing. Point to an object or anything in front of you with your finger.

2.Notice the object which your finger is pointing. You may say the thing that you have pointed or just observe for 30 seconds. This object is not part of your body.

3. Now you need to point your finger to your feet. This is a part of your body

And watch it for a few seconds or minimum 30 seconds.

4. Now point your finger at your chest area.

Notice your chest part. It is a part of your body

5. Now slowly move your finger up forward towards your face above your chest where you can no longer see anything or any part

6. Now suddenly point your finger directly in front of eyes

7. Note what your finger is pointing at. You won't be able to explain what you are pointing at.

Now you are really pointing at your consciousness.

This experience will be of pointing to nothingness. Enlightenment is an experience that you are not a thing. The experience of nothingness liberates you from thingness.

If you experience this be in it. Be it for some time initially and later you will experience in everything you do.

It is not fictious, it is a reality which is already present in everyone. Just we never look in.

The mind will not have an experience with which it can validate it. As this experience cannot be captured by the mind and hence cannot be explained but only experienced.

When you are out of the mind, watching it, being aware of it, just being a witness, you are intelligent.

Your intelligence is discovered.

You have undone what society has done to you. You have destroyed the wrong done by the priest and politicians.

You have come out of it and are free.

Concept 95 - How to be enlightened - Part 1

To become enlightened, one has to be reborn in this same life in the sense one has to have a psychological death.

A death in which you are devoid of your ego, your identity as a person of various qualities. One has to be reborn as a new spiritual being.

You need to let go of all the conditioning, it may be from your parents, teachers, priests, politicians, it may be from your friend or from anyone.

Your parents or people around you, or the media around you. They are not enlightened people, naturally you will listen to all the things which is against being enlightened. And to fit in the society you may adopt the views. Your parents teach you with good intentions, but when they themselves are trapped, then how can they give you the right directions.

Their parents have not given them directions
and so on it goes when human beings started.

Concept 96 - How to be enlightened - Part 2

You were born as a child with nothing in your mind, with certain predefined strong traits genetically and by the combination of astrological stars you got developed in a way different from other people. I am not explaining here how you get developed astrologically. It's a vast topic.

You were told you were Christian, Hindu, Muslim. You came into the world with nothing. You were told about sin, hell and heaven, so that you follow the road of virtue and a God of faith sitting above you. Nothing wrong with the intentions, but a person who himself is trapped, cannot really guide.

Concept 97 - How to be enlightened - Part 3

Fear of losing the conditioning.

You may have developed a certain personality. Maybe you are a good sportsman, a singer, good in academics, maybe good looking, maybe well behaved, maybe creative, maybe a painter, maybe a good son, maybe a good daughter, maybe very scientific, maybe good with boys, maybe good with the girls, maybe intelligent or less intelligent, maybe strong or weak.

If you can see in all this, people have an opinion about you and you are made of the opinions of others.

This is the condoning which you have to lose. But you are afraid to lose it. Because the very idea of you will be in stake.

The very idea of "I" will be at stake. Lose yourself and you will find yourself.

The personality which is dependent on this you need to get rid of this. You need to be just like what you were in your mother's womb totally free, without even a name.

Watch when any thoughts come, what is the base of it, why is it there, what is the root cause of it, just don't think it is you who are thinking. It is but a combination of things which has given you these thoughts. Think from zero to the thought you are thinking why are you thinking that way.

Concept 98 - How to be enlightened - Part 4

When the personality dies, you don't need to be enlightened. You are automatically enlightened.

You are in awe of yourself, what you do, what you are doing, what you have done. You think you have done great things or will do great things.

You may think that you have some qualities, some talent, some things which you are good at and some things which you are bad at. This is your ego. This is all that makes your ego with characters of unique personality.

Once you drop this personality the pure self which is watching, appears.

At first you are in awe of what is enlightenment. As you have achieved other things in life you may want to put effort and achieve it as you must have done some other great things.

But here you cannot do it. The very idea that "I" am doing it has to be dropped. And when you drop the I and what it wants to achieve you will reach it. I have seen there are some people who have all the riches of life in the world, think enlightenment is a trophy to be achieved and want to show to people.

But the very fact that they want to be enlightened for the wrong reasons, puts a hindrance as enlightenment is not possible without dissolving oneself.

It will require the death of personality for whoever are not enlightened and then they can return to the self or spirit.

Concept 99 - How to be enlightened - Part 5

Like an onion peeling, peel the layers in life.

What I have seen is the people who are enlightened generally happen at a very young age around 18 to 25 years. Somehow their personalities are not very strong at this age. They are still developing and don't have a lot of baggage to remove and have a certain momentum which they carry from their past lives which makes them enlightened. They may have not read any books but still, somehow, they start questioning life as soon as they get a setback. They will ask, who am I, why I was born, where I was born, where I was before birth, why this type of birth, all these questions they want answers and they do get it.

Whereas for others who are seeking enlightenment at a later stage of life where they are in a mist of storm or very much active in their life. Maybe they are married, having kids it really become difficult for them, to lose their personality, they need to observe each and every aspect of life layer by layer of why they have developed a certain personality.

Existence has happened randomly without any reason and randomly there was never a starting point, it existed always.

If you were enlightened previously and randomly you become unenlightened, so can you become enlightened again randomly. There was no reason you had to become unenlightened. You don't need to exhaust all your sins or karmas and then you become enlightened. Should not be that way.

If you seek or if you desire you can become enlightened. But you need to understand yourself. When your personality dissolves to zero and then the real self comes out.

Firstly, you can desire enlightenment, after some time, even that desire has to be given up.

At first you should have the desire to be enlightened, then only you may give up layers or desires of your personality.

Only at a later stage, even the desire to be enlightened has to be given up.

When you slowly peel off all personality, and lastly only the desire to be enlightened remains even that also needs to be given up where the "I" is dissolved. If you first give up the desire to become enlightened without peeling up the layers, you may not achieve anything.

Concept 100 - How to be enlightened - Part 6. Fear of losing your personality

You don't know what you will get by losing your personality.

For a person who is enlightened can tell what is there after you lose your personality.

But a person who is not enlightened and becomes extremely difficult to give up things.

As the mind thinks in terms of profit and loss, by losing your personality, you may seem that you are losing entirely and gain nothing. And by the way, what are you losing, you always seems to be in thoughts of sex, boredom, despair, failure, house of complexity, you seem to be filled with boredom. Why are you bored, why is the mind always fulfilling things with something, why can't the mind relax as it is, why the mind always wants something.

You need to embrace the emptiness with you and not get bored by it. Because it is you, your very nature, if you get bored by impulses then you are bored with yourself. It is the trick of the mind as the mind is diametrically opposite to your real self.

Mind wants to fulfill all the things actively whereas your real self just watches and is stable.

If you have children, can you say I give up my children.

If you are talented, a great singer, can you give up your ambition.

If you are a social worker, can you give up the charity.

Whatever you do can you really give it up.

The thought of giving up only may be troublesome for you.

Just give up and do a psychological suicide and will become detached and suddenly you will be in a bliss which was always there with you and you will be much clearer and the bliss will rest in you.

Take a jump into knowing yourself and I will happen. It is not your worldly life is over. But to reach a sage of enlightenment you need to go beyond worldly life.

 **Concept 101 - It's really strange, your past lives are hidden from you.**

It's really strange, your past lives are hidden from you. Why is it hidden from you, is it because you don't want to get a headache thinking about your past, as you may be already exhausted in your old age. It could be that existence got created without any reason for it, it is its very nature.

Now dynamically, it's just nature, it happens on its own nobody must have created. Maybe in Hindu books they said Brahma is the creator, but who created Brahma and if somebody created Brahma why did it got created or in Bible its said Yahweh created in

7 days, but who created Yahweh. Well, the simple truth is the existence or the entire world is automatic. Nobody can tell the start point of creation. Just as you think God is ultimate, why can't you think the existence is eternally moving and we are part of it.

Electricity powers various instruments in different shapes. Similarly, so does the eternal energy also power every living being.

+

Concept 102 - Who attains perfection

Now who really attains perfection.

Attaining transcendental knowledge, one who has purified his intellect attains perfection.

In the sense one whose thinking remains neutral and is not driven by the driving mind can become neutral, is automatically purified and takes the right decision every time.

People who can see the mind working don't need to subdue it, as the intellect will be supreme to the mind and will always take the right decision automatically. They can drive away from the forceful power of the mind, its likes and dislikes.

These people can also be alone just living in the self.

Fully satisfied will the self, controlling the mind, speech and organs these people take refuge in the self, devoid of any ego and false notation of I and become peaceful, and know the supreme.

Concept 103 - Set aside all meretricious deeds

One needs to go beyond the things a person has achieved and wants to achieve. As when you think you have achieved, there will always be something more to achieve in the material world. There is no end to this. It's very tiring and doesn't give you rest.

You need to explore that there is something beyond which is better. One doesn't know what it is but one needs to take a gamble and dive into it. You may never do it as for the logical mind, its beyond interpretation. Hence, just dive into it and see the truth.

Also go beyond the rituals and first focus on the infinite invisible energy or whatever you may give a name to it. Slowly and steadily the power will help you get closer to it. And help you from all sins and make you enlightened.

Concept 104 - There is no pilgrimage

A person should seek enlightenment, because without seeking existence, it will not happen

But later there should be no pilgrimage or seeking. Because in the very seeking the person will miss.

Seeking is when the truth is far away and there should be no seeking when the truth is right here. You are the truth, inside you is the truth, the power that powers everything which is in the present is the truth.

Seeking is a desire.

To have desire is to have the mind active.

To have the mind inactive and to go beyond is to know the reality.

You seek what you don't have, but the truth is always there and it is in the present. Truth is found when you are not.

Truth and you cannot be at the same time.

If you didn't get the truth, you are still there. When you are there, you will go on missing it.

It is not a question of how to be, but it is a question of how not to be. The moment we desire not to be, it happens.

Seeking you turn towards the sky. God is far away. It seems to be a very long journey.

It is wrong to think Only great people famous saints can reach enlightenment. You may not know how many people have reached enlightenment except for the famous ones who have been teachers. This is all false. God is right now in you, powers you just like electricity powers different devices.

The truth is close very close in fact it's so close, that the truth is you. You yourself are the one you are seeking.

Concept 105 - Seeking the continuous God

You can seek something if you have known it. You can set a target a goal.

How is it possible to seek something which you don't know? You really cannot set a target or goal. Because you don't know where is the goal or what is the goal.

People who are guided by religious priests, they themselves have not reached, but they assume that God is in a certain way, which they tell people.

Priest create a dream of God. They create an illusion of God or dream, and seek.

If tomorrow the real God comes to you, you won't be able to believe because you are made up of your priest, and you decide by your past. In dreams you don't doubt anything. Suddenly there is a dog, and it turns into a cat, you don't question it.

In dreams you accept everything.

The ability to create anything of a person is tremendous.

Even great logicians are fooled in their dream and in the morning when they wake up, they realize what a fool they were.

This is the same case in real life, you do similarly in real life and accept everything but once you wake up you actually come to know the reality. Mind is made by our past experiences, which is very limited, when you seek, you seek the imagination which you have created.

Concept 106 - There is nothing to seek

There is nothing to seek. An enlightened person knows there is nothing to seek, as you are already there. Nothing needs to be attained

But for common unenlightened people they need to have a goal or seek a goal. Then a point comes when they need to drop the seeking as well.

When they drop, they know they have realized.

When Jesus Christ says "seek and you will find", he is talking to fishers, carpenters etc. They have just started, for them its ok, but for an advance person who has kept on finding. He needs to drop that as well.

Seeking means concentration acts, truth cannot be found by concentration or focus

Truth is achieved when your mind is not focused.

Truth is achieved by observing or meditating. Really mediation is not focusing but defocusing

An unenlightened man has been a person who claims to be expert go on telling that meditation is concentration.

In fact, meditation or enlightenment is really opposite. By releasing the focus and not focusing you can achieve the ultimate bliss.

Spread the world

Spread the world if you have learned about the spirit, teach it to others and you will get better.

ACKNOWLEDGMENTS

I would like to give credit to all the inspiration from Bhagavat Gita, Bible, Osho, Jainism, Buddhism, Zen. J.Krishnamurthy. Shiv Samhita an many more

I have gone through a lot of work in case I missed to mention anyone do excuse me.

ABOUT THE AUTHOR

Franklin Manickam is one of India's' modern age enlightened master. Having studied various spiritual text. He has made an attempt to take it to the next level 0f spiritual understanding. There were many Gurus who showed the right path. But the path can be made better and better in understanding. His attempt is to take spiritual knowledge to the next level. Each generation does produces people who take forward knowledge which even better than the previous enlightened masters.

One needs to have an open view and not limit ourselves to think openly without any crutches. He in his books, videos and spiritual sessions wants to do exactly that.

If you have any queries or want to reach out email on info@franklinmanickam.com

Index

A

B

C

D

E

ego, 10, 29, 30, 56, 63, 64, 67, 69, 76, 82, 108, 138, 139, 144, 146, 159, 164, 174

enlightenment, 3, 1, 5, 6, 7, 9, 10, 26, 28, 29, 30, 38, 47, 49, 52, 81, 82, 90, 91, 95, 109, 116, 126, 128, 131, 164, 165, 166, 168, 176, 177, 181

F

family, 2, 6, 10, 15, 17, 18, 19, 109, 137

Foreword, 1

G

God, 28, 30, 31, 43, 45, 80, 85, 100, 103, 119, 125, 141, 161, 172, 177, 178

Goodness, 84, 105, 124

I

Ignorance, 84, 108, 121

Intellect, 64, 65

K

knowledge, 2, 5, 6, 7, 8, 10, 48, 57, 60, 62, 71, 75, 77, 83, 85, 90, 95, 115, 145, 146, 173, 183

L

living, 15, 58, 66, 72, 75, 76, 80, 87, 96, 97, 99, 121, 127, 145, 172, 173

lust, 10, 21, 22, 39, 40, 41, 61, 120

M

master, 25, 26, 27, 47, 123, 183
material, 10, 33, 35, 43, 48, 53, 55, 62, 64, 66, 67, 69, 70, 71, 72, 75, 76, 84, 85, 86, 99, 104, 107, 109, 110, 115, 119, 120, 123, 175
Matter, 64, 96
mind, 1, 3, 6, 14, 16, 17, 21, 22, 23, 24, 25, 26, 27, 29, 31, 33, 37, 38, 39, 40, 41, 50, 55, 56, 58, 59, 60, 61, 62, 63, 64, 65, 67, 68, 76, 79, 80, 81, 82, 84, 87, 90, 93, 95, 96, 101, 104, 105, 107, 109, 112, 113, 117, 119, 126, 133, 135, 136, 142, 143, 144, 161, 169, 170, 173, 175, 176, 179, 181
Mind, 55, 64, 170

N

Nature, 34, 44, 51, 53, 60, 105
Nirvana, 83

P

Passion, 84, 145
past, 2, 7, 9, 15, 19, 23, 29, 31, 48, 49, 55, 57, 60, 62, 63, 64, 65, 87, 90, 112, 145, 166, 171, 178, 179
past life, 9, 15, 49, 87, 112
People, 10, 14, 30, 35, 43, 45, 60, 69, 76, 80, 85, 86, 124, 128, 132, 145, 173, 178
perfection, 37, 62, 90, 173

Q

qualities, 11, 75, 82, 96, 116, 121, 124, 125, 136, 159, 164

R

ritualistic, 44, 73, 123
rituals, 30, 33, 43, 44, 48, 99, 175

S

W

Glossary

Attachment	Can be defined as a deep and enduring emotional bond between two people or craving and being bond to a material thing like money achievement.
Austerity	Sternness or severity of manner or attitude towards a particular task
Biological	Of or relating to biology or to life and living processes
Brahma	The creator god of the Hindu
Cause and effect	Cause-and-effect describes a relationship between actions or events in which at least one action or event is a direct result of the others
Celibacy	The state of abstaining from marriage and sexual relations
Charity	The voluntary giving of help, typically in the form of money, to those in need
Conviction	A firmly held belief or opinion
Deity	A god or goddess
Detachments	Someone who is detached is not personally involved in something or has no emotional interest in it
Ego	An ego is a person's sense of self-esteem or self-importance. To have an ego is essential to our very makeup. It will define who we are and how we connect with others. Ego becomes an issue when it becomes overpowering. Everyone has an ego, whether big or small.
Equanimity	Evenness of mind especially under

	stress nothing could disturb his equanimity
Ethical	Pertaining to or dealing with morals or the principles of morality; pertaining to right and wrong in conduct. Being in accordance with the rules or standards for right conduct or practice, 116 Five senses - faculties of sight, touch, smell, taste and hearing
Formless	Having no regular form or shape, that which cannot be imagined or seen
Gita	The Shrimad Bhagavad Gita, often referred to as the Gita, is a 700-verse Hindu scripture that is part of the epic Mahabharata, dated to the second half of the first millennium BCE and is typical of the Hindu synthesis. It is considered to be one of the holy scriptures for Hinduism.
Goodness	The quality of being morally good or virtuous.
Guru	An influential teacher or popular expert
Ignorance	Ignorance is a lack of knowledge and information. The word "ignorant" is an adjective that describes a person in the state of being unaware, or even cognitive dissonance and other cognitive relation, and can describe individuals who are unaware of important information or facts.
Inquisitive	Having or showing an interest in learning things; curious.
Intellect	The faculty of reasoning and

	understanding objectively, especially with regard to abstract matters.
Karmas	(in Hinduism and Buddhism) the sum of a person's actions in this and previous states of existence, viewed as deciding their fate in future existences.
Lust	Usually intense or unbridled sexual desire
Mantras	(Originally in Hinduism and Buddhism) a word or sound repeated to aid concentration in meditation.
Material	The matter from which a thing is or can be made.
Maya	The power by which the universe becomes manifest; the illusion or appearance of the phenomenal world.
Mind	The part of a person that thinks, reasons, feels, understands, and remembers
Modes of Nature	Material nature is expressed, and thus, perceived through these qualities. The Gita categorizes these qualities into three primary modes: goodness (sattva-Guna), passion (raja-Guna), and ignorance (tama-guna)
Nectar	A sugary fluid secreted within flowers to encourage pollination by insects and other animals, collected by bees to make into honey.
Next life	A life that is believed by some people to come after death
Non-delusion	Having false or unrealistic beliefs or opinions
Notation	The act, process, method, or an instance of representing by a system or set of marks, signs, figures, or

	characters
Passion	Strong and barely controllable emotion. 94
Peeling	Remove the outer covering or skin from (a fruit or vegetable).
Personality	The combination of characteristics or qualities that form an individual's distinctive character.
Pujas	Puja, also spelled pooja or poojah, in Hinduism, ceremonial worship, ranging from brief daily rites in the home to elaborate temple rituals48 Scriptures - books of various religions
Self	A person's essential being that distinguishes them from others, especially considered as the object of introspection or reflexive action.
Senses	A faculty by which the body perceives an external stimulus; one of the faculties of sight, smell, hearing, taste, and touch.
Sexuality	Sexuality is about your sexual feelings, thoughts, attractions and behaviors towards other people
Spirit	The non-physical part of a person 10 Steadfastness - the quality of being resolutely or dutifully firm and unwavering
Supreme	Highest in rank or authority.
Upanishads	The Sanskrit term Upanishad (from upa "by" and ni-ṣad "sit down") translates to "sitting down near", referring to the student sitting down near the teacher while receiving spiritual knowledge.

Yahweh	A form of the Hebrew name of God used in the Bible.